AUTHENTIC CHORDS
ORIGINAL KEYS
COMPLETE SONGS

BEST OF
WOODY GUTHRIE

Photo courtesy of Howard Greenberg Gallery, NYC
Copyright Miriam Grossman

Arranged by Mick O'Brien

ISBN-13: 978-0-6340-3587-6
ISBN-10: 0-634-03587-8

Ludlow Music, Inc.

 The Richmond Organization

EXCLUSIVELY DISTRIBUTED BY

HAL•LEONARD®
CORPORATION
7777 W. BLUEMOUND RD. P.O. BOX 13819 MILWAUKEE, WI 53213

Visit Hal Leonard Online at
www.halleonard.com

BEST OF

WOODY GUTHRIE

Contents

HOW TO USE THIS BOOK

Strum It is the series designed especially to get you playing (and singing!) along with your favorite songs. The idea is simple—the songs are arranged using their original keys in lead sheet format, giving you the chords for each song, beginning to end. The melody and lyrics are also shown to help you keep your spot and sing along.

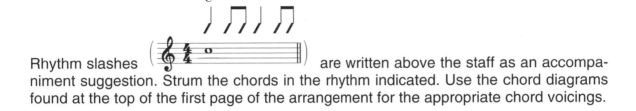

Rhythm slashes are written above the staff as an accompaniment suggestion. Strum the chords in the rhythm indicated. Use the chord diagrams found at the top of the first page of the arrangement for the appropriate chord voicings.

Additional Musical Definitions

⊓	• Downstroke
∨	• Upstroke
D.S. al Coda	• Go back to the sign (𝄋), then play until the measure marked *"To Coda,"* then skip to the section labelled *"Coda."*
D.C. al Fine	• Go back to the beginning of the song and play until the measure marked *"Fine"* (end).
cont. rhy. sim.	• Continue using similar rhythm pattern.
N.C.	• Instrument is silent (drops out).
𝄆 𝄇	• Repeat measures between signs.
1. 2.	• When a repeated section has different endings, play the first ending only the first time and the second ending only the second time.

Deportee
(Plane Wreck at Los Gatos)

Words by Woody Guthrie
Music by Martin Hoffman

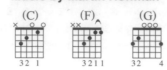

* Symbols in parentheses represent chord names respective to capoed guitar.
  Symbols above reflect actual sounding chords.

A - di - os   mi a - mi - go,   Je - sus and Ma -

ri - a. _____   You   won't   have   a   name   when   you ___

ride   the   big   air - plane,   and   all   they   will

call   you   will   be _____   de - por - tee.

2. My   tee.

Additional Lyrics

2. My father's own father, he waded that river.
   They took all the money he made in his life.
   My brothers and sisters come working the fruit trees,
   And they rode on the trucks till they took down and died.

3. Well, some are illegal, and some are not wanted.
   Our work contract's out and we've got to move on.
   Six hundred miles to that Mexico border;
   They chased us like outlaws, like rustlers, like thieves.

4. We died in your hills, and we died on your deserts;
   We died in your valleys, we died on your plains.
   We died 'neath your trees and we died in your bushes.
   Both sides of that river, we died just the same.

5. The sky plane caught fire over Los Gatos canyon,
   Like a fireball of lightning, and shook all our hills.
   Who are all these friends, all scattered like dry leaves?
   The radio says they are just deportees.

6. Is this the best way we can grow our big orchards?
   Is this the best way we can grow our good fruit?
   To fall like dry leaves and rot on my topsoil,
   And be known by no name except deportee.

Do Re Mi

Words and Music by Woody Guthrie

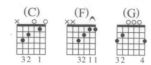

Capo IV

Verse
Fast

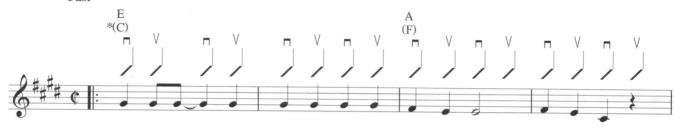

1. Lots of folks_ back east they say is leav - in' home ev - 'ry day,
2. *See additional lyrics*

* Symbols in parentheses represent chord names respective to capoed guitar.
  Symbols above reflect actual sounding chords.

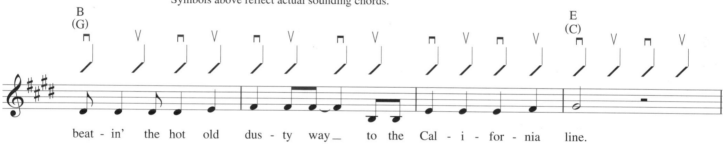

beat - in' the hot old dus - ty way_ to the Cal - i - for - nia line.

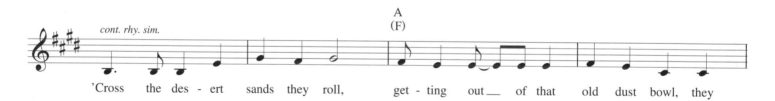

'Cross the des - ert sands they roll, get - ting out_ of that old dust bowl, they

think they're go - ing to a su - gar bowl,_ but here is what they find:

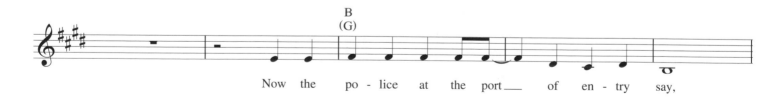

Now the po - lice at the port_ of en - try say,

"You're num - ber four - teen thou - sand for to - day." Oh, if you

Chorus

ain't got the do, re, mi, folks, if you ain't got the
do, re, mi,_____ why, you bet-ter go back,__ to
beau - ti - ful Tex - as, Ok - la - ho - ma, Kan - sas,
Geor - gia, Ten - nes - see.__ Cal - i - for - nia is a gar - den of
E - den, a par - a - dise__ to live in or see,
but be - lieve it or not you won't find it so hot, if you
ain't got the do, re, mi. mi.

Additional Lyrics

2. If you want to buy you a home or farm
   That can't deal nobody harm,
   Or take your vacation by the mountains or sea,
   Don't swap your old cow for a car;
   You'd better stay right where you are.
   You'd better take this little tip from me.
   'Cause I look through the want ads ev'ry day,
   But the headlines on the papers always say:

Dust Pneumonia Blues

Words and Music by Woody Guthrie

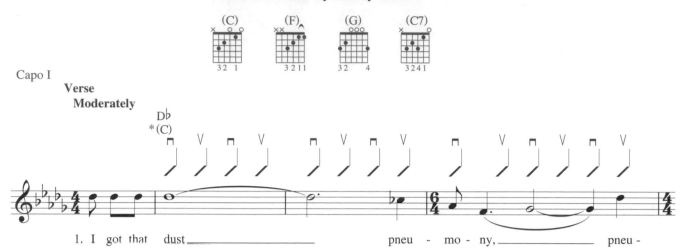

Capo I

Verse
Moderately

1. I got that dust _____ pneu - mo - ny, _____ pneu -

* Symbols in parentheses represent chord names respective to capoed guitar.
Symbols above reflect actual sounding chords.

mo - ny in my lung. I got the dust pneu -

mo - ny, pneu - mo - ny in my lung. And

I'm a gon - na sing _____ this dust pneu - mo - ny song. 2. I

Verse

went to the doc - tor, and the doc - tor said, "My son."

3.-7. See additional lyrics

Additional Lyrics

3. Now there ought to be some yodelin' in this song,
   And there ought to be some yodelin' in this song,
   But I can't yodel for the rattlin' in my lung.

4. My good gal sings the dust pneumony blues.
   My good gal sings the dust pneumony blues.
   She loves me 'cause she's got the dust pneumony too.

5. If it wasn't for choppin' my hoe would turn to rust.
   If it wasn't for choppin' my hoe would turn to rust.
   I can't find a woman in this black old Texas dust.

6. Down in Oklahoma the wind blows mighty strong.
   Down in Oklahoma the wind blows mighty strong.
   If you want to get a mama, just sing a California song.

7. Down in Texas my gal fainted in the rain.
   Down in Texas my gal fainted in the rain.
   I throwed a bucket of dirt in her face just to bring her back again.

Going Down the Road
(I Ain't Going to Be Treated This Way)

Words and Music by Woody Guthrie and Lee Hays

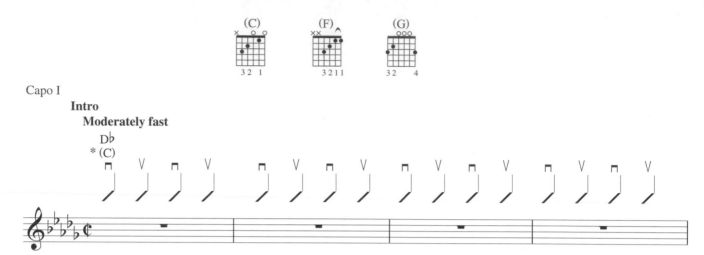

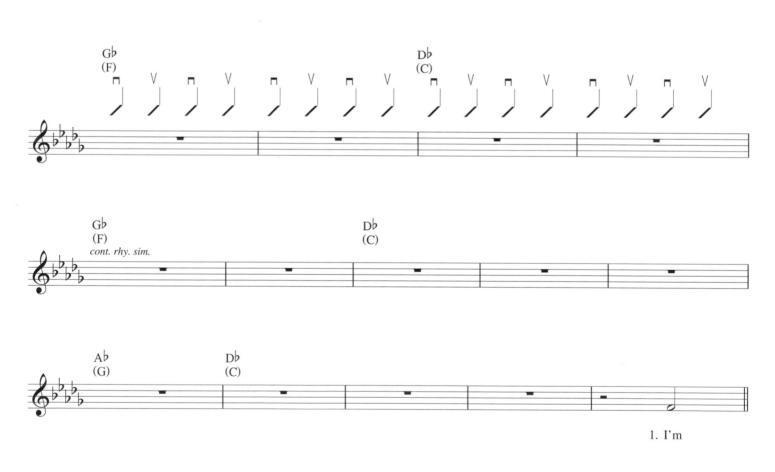

Capo I

* Symbols in parentheses represent chord names respective to capoed guitar.
  Symbols above reflect actual sounding chords.

blow-in' down this old dus-ty road. _____ I'm a

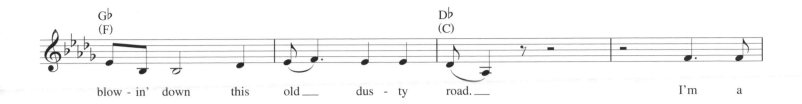

blow - in' down this old ___ dus - ty road. ___ I'm a

blow - in' down ___ this old dus - ty road, Lord, Lord, and I

ain't a gon - na be treat - ed this way. 2. I'm a

Verse

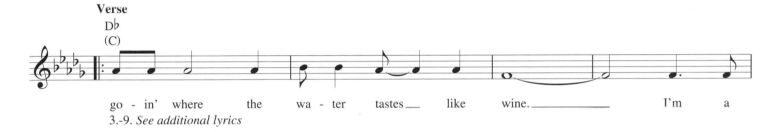

go - in' where the wa - ter tastes ___ like wine. ___ I'm a
3.-9. *See additional lyrics*

go - in' where the wa - ter tastes ___ like wine. I'm a

go - in' where ___ the wa - ter tastes ___ like wine, Lord, and I

|1.-7.

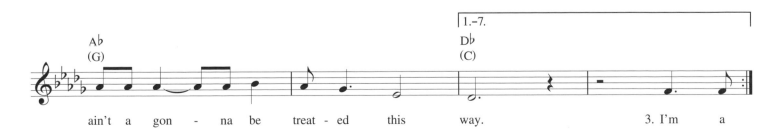

ain't a gon - na be treat - ed this way. 3. I'm a

way.

grad. rit.

Additional Lyrics

3. I'm a goin' where the dust storms never blow.
   I'm a goin' where them a dust storms never blow.
   I'm a goin' where them dust storms never blow, blow, blow
   And I ain't a gonna be treated this way.

4. They say I'm a dust bowl refugee.
   Yes, they say I'm a dust bowl refugee.
   They say I'm a dust bowl refugee, Lord, Lord,
   But I ain't a gonna be treated this way.

5. I'm a lookin' for a job at honest pay.
   I'm a lookin' for a job at honest pay.
   I'm a lookin' for a job at honest pay, Lord, Lord,
   And I ain't a gonna be treated this way.

6. My children need three square meals a day.
   Now, my children need three square meals a day.
   My children need three square meals a day, Lord,
   And I ain't a gonna be treated this way.

7. It takes a ten dollar shoe to fit my feet.
   It takes a ten dollar shoe to fit my feet.
   It takes a ten dollar shoe to fit my feet, Lord, Lord,
   And I ain't a gonna be treated this way.

8. Your a two dollar shoe hurts my feet.
   Your two dollar shoe hurts my feet.
   Yes, your two dollar shoe hurts my feet, Lord, Lord,
   And I ain't a gonna be treated this way.

9. I'm a goin' down this old dusty road.
   I'm blowin' down this old dusty road.
   I'm a blowin' down this old dusty road, Lord, Lord,
   And I ain't a gonna be treated this way.

I Ain't Got No Home

Words and Music by Woody Guthrie

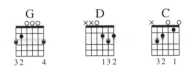

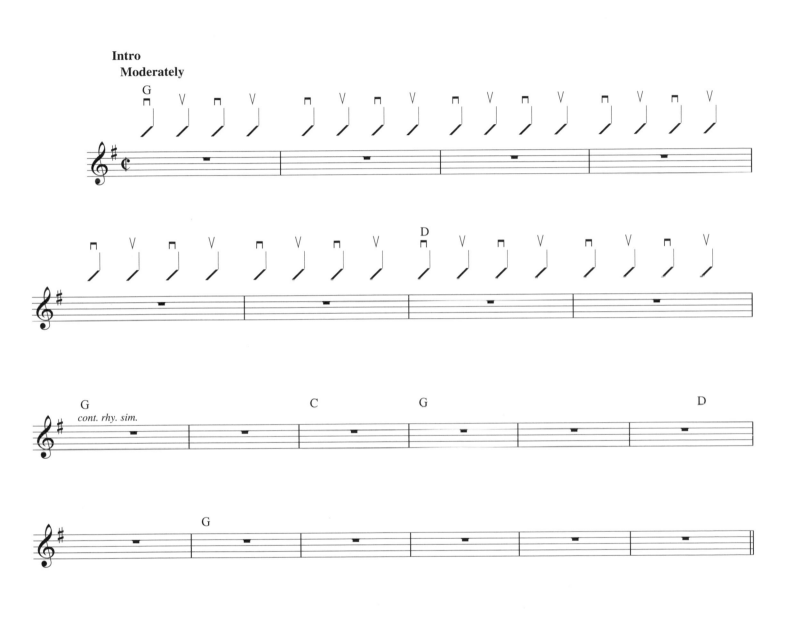

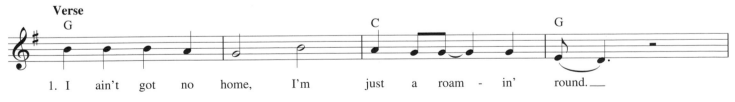

Verse

1. I ain't got no home, I'm just a roam-in' round. ___ Just a wan-d'rin' work-er, I go from town to town. And the

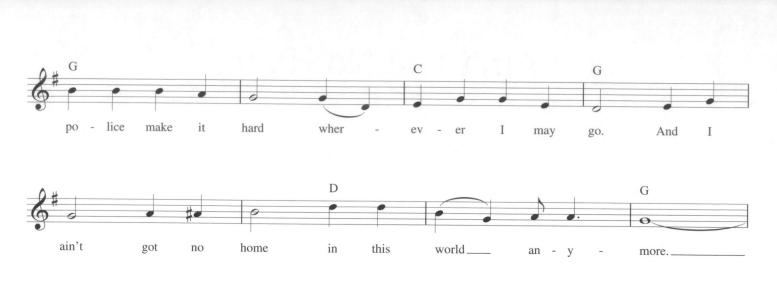

po - lice make it hard wher - ev - er I may go. And I

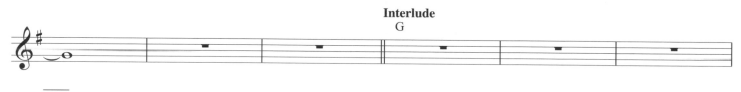

ain't got no home in this world ___ an - y - more. ___

Interlude

𝄉 **Verse**

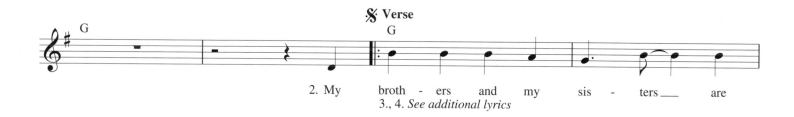

2. My broth - ers and my sis - ters ___ are
3., 4. *See additional lyrics*

strand - ed on ___ this road. ___ A hot and dust - y road that a

mil - lion feet have trod. Rich man took my

Additional Lyrics

3. Was a farmin' on the shares
   And always I was poor.
   My crops I lay into the banker's store.
   My wife took down and died
   Upon the cabin floor.
   And I ain't got no home in this world anymore.

4. Now as I look around
   It's mighty plain to see,
   This world is such a great and a funny place to be.
   All the gambling man is rich
   And the workin' man is poor.
   And I ain't got no home in this world anymore.

The Grand Coulee Dam

Words and Music by Woody Guthrie
Melody based on a traditional theme

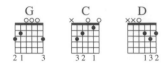

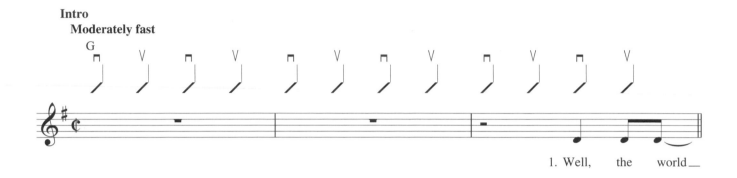

Intro
Moderately fast

1. Well, the world___

Verse

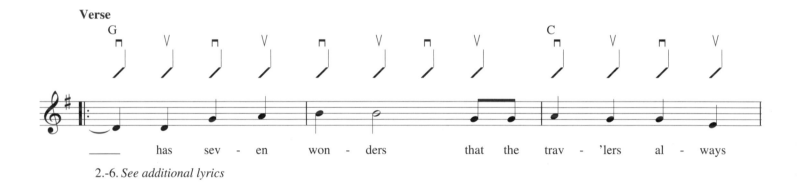

_____ has sev - en won - ders that the trav - 'lers al - ways

2.-6. See additional lyrics

tell, some gar - dens and some tow - ers, I

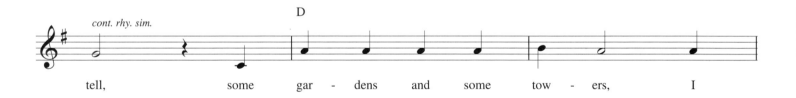

guess you know them well. But now the great - est

won - der is in Un - cle Sam's fair land, it's that

king Co - lum - bia Riv - er and the big Grand___ Cou - lee Dam.

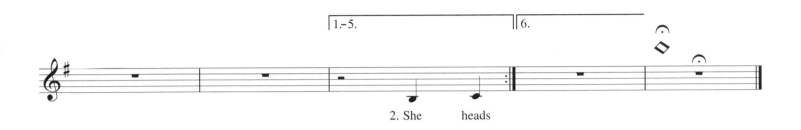

2. She heads

Additional Lyrics

2.   She heads up the Canadian Rockies where the rippling waters glide,
Comes a rumbling down the canyon to meet that salty tide,
Of the wide Pacific Ocean where the sun sets in the West
And the big Grand Coulee country in the land I love the best.

3.,6. In the misty crystal glitter of that wild and wind ward spray,
Men have fought the pounding waters and met a watery grave.
Well, she tore their boats to splinters, but she gave men dreams to dream
Of the day the Coulee Dam went across that wild and wasted stream.

4.   Uncle Sam took up the challenge in the year of 'thirty-three,
For the farmer and the factory and all of you and me.
He said, "Roll along, Columbia, you can ramble to the sea,
But river, while you're ramblin' you can do some work for me."

5.   Now in Washington and Oregon you hear the factories hum,
Makin' chrome and makin' manganese and light aluminum.
And there roars the flying fortress now to fight for Uncle Sam,
Spawned upon the King Columbia by the big Grand Coulee Dam.

Hard Travelin'

Words and Music by Woody Guthrie

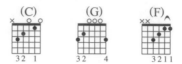

Capo II

Intro
Moderately fast

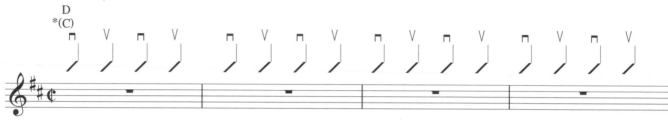

* Symbols in parentheses represent chord names respective to capoed guitar.
Symbols above reflect actual sounding chords.

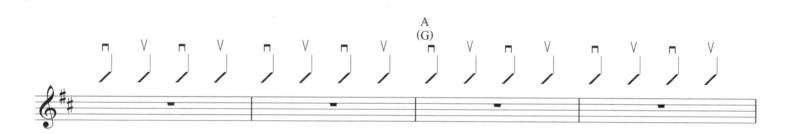

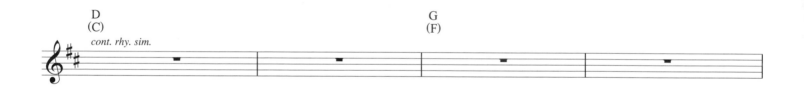

Verse

1. I've been hav-in' some hard trav-el-in', I thought you knowed,
2.-7. *See additional lyrics*

I've been hav-in' some hard trav-el-in' way down the road. ___

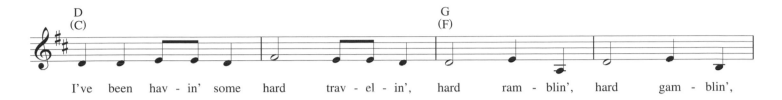

I've been hav-in' some hard trav-el-in', hard ram-blin', hard gam-blin',

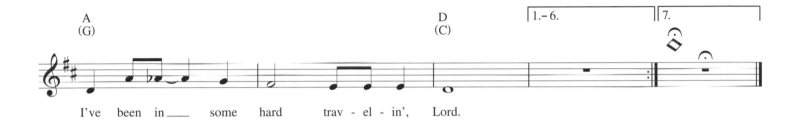

I've been in ___ some hard trav-el-in', Lord.

Additional Lyrics

2. I've been a-ridin' them fast rattlers, I thought you knowed,
   I've been a-ridin' them flat wheelers way down the road.
   I've been a-ridin' them dead enders, blind passengers, kickin' up cinders,
   I've been a-havin' some hard travelin', Lord.

3. Well, I've been a-hitting some hard rock mining, I thought you knowed,
   I've been a-leaning on a pressure drill way down the road;
   Hammer flyin', air hose suckin', six foot of mud and I sure been a-muckin',
   And I've been a-havin' some hard travelin', Lord.

4. Well, I've been a-hittin' some hard harvestin', I thought you knowed,
   North Dakota to Kansas City way down the road.
   Cutting that wheat and stackin' that hay, and I'm tryin' to make about a dollar a day,
   And I've been a-havin' some hard travelin', Lord.

5. I've been a-working that Pittsburgh steel, I thought you knowed,
   I've been a-pourin' red-hot slag way down the road.
   I've been blastin', I've been firin', and I've been pourin' red-hot iron,
   And I've been a-havin' some hard travelin', Lord.

6. Well, I've been layin' in a hard rock jail, I thought you knowed,
   I've been layin' out ninety days way down the road.
   Mean old judge he said to me, "It's ninety days for vagrancy,"
   And I've been a-hittin' some hard travelin', Lord.

7. Well, I've been walkin' that Lincoln highway, I thought you knowed,
   I've been a-hittin' that Sixty-Six way down the road.
   Heavy load and a worried mind, lookin' for a woman that's hard to find,
   And I've been a-hittin' some hard travelin', Lord.

I've Got to Know

Words and Music by Woody Guthrie

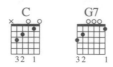

Moderately

℀ **Chorus**

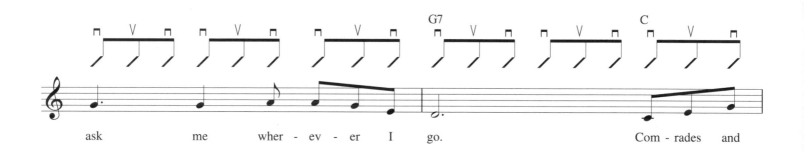

I've got to know, yes, I've got to know, friend. Hun-gry lips

ask me wher-ev-er I go. Com-rades and

friends all fall-ing a-round me, I've got to know, yes, I've got to

Verse

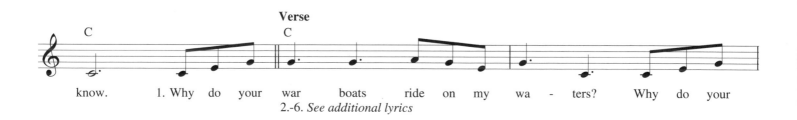

know. 1. Why do your war boats ride on my wa-ters? Why do your

2.-6. *See additional lyrics*

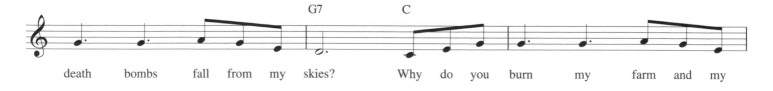

death bombs fall from my skies? Why do you burn my farm and my

town   down?   I've   got   to   know,   friend,   I've   got   to   know.   I've   got   to

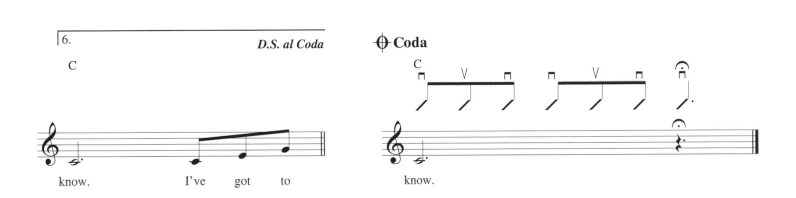

6.

D.S. al Coda

Coda

know.   I've   got   to   know.

Additional Lyrics

2. What makes your boats haul death to my people?
   Nitro blockbusters, big cannons and guns?
   Why doesn't your ship bring food and some clothing?
   I've sure got to know, folks, I've sure got to know.

3. Why can't my two hands get a good pay job?
   I can still plow, plant, I can still sow!
   Why did your lawbook chase me off my good land?
   I'd sure like to know, friend, I've just got to know.

4. What good work did you do, sir, I'd like to ask you,
   To give you my money right out of my hands?
   I built your big house here to hide from my people.
   Why you crave to hide so, I'd love to know.

5. You keep me in jail and you lock me in prison.
   Your hospital's jammed and your crazyhouse full.
   What made your cop kill my trade union worker?
   You'll have to talk plain 'cause I sure have to know.

6. Why can't I get work and cash my big paycheck?
   Why can't I buy things in your place and your store?
   Why do you close my plant down and starve all my buddies?
   I'm asking you, sir, 'cause I've sure got to know.

Jackhammer John

Words and New Music Adaptation by Woody Guthrie

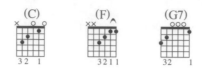

Capo II

Verse
Moderately

1. Jack - ham - mer John was a jack - ham - mer man. Born with a jack - ham - mer
2.-6. *See additional lyrics*

* Symbols in parentheses represent chord names respective to capoed guitar.
  Symbols above reflect actual sounding chords.

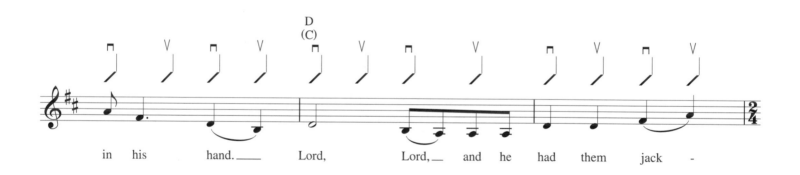

in his hand.___ Lord, Lord,___ and he had them jack -

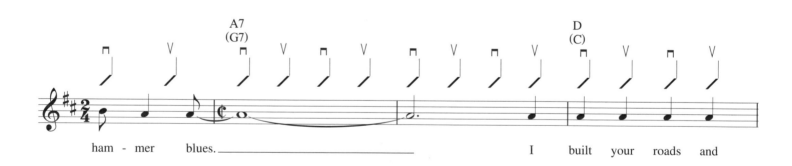

ham - mer blues._____ I built your roads and

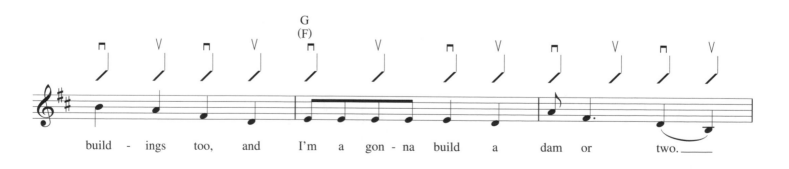

build - ings too, and I'm a gon - na build a dam or two.___

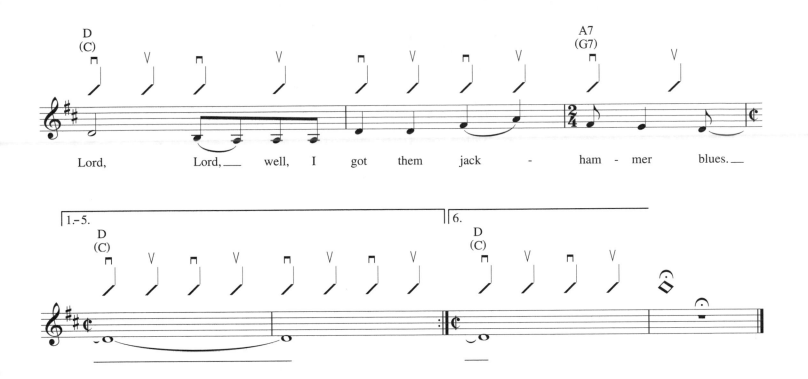

Lord,   Lord,___ well,   I   got   them   jack - ham - mer   blues.___

Additional Lyrics

2. I was borned in Portland town,
   Built every port from Alasky down.
   Lord, Lord, and he had them jackhammer blues.
   Built your bridges, dug your mines;
   Been in jail a thousand times.
   Lord, Lord, well, I got them jackhammer blues.

3. Jackhammer, Jackhammer, where you been?
   Been out a chasin' them gals again.
   Lord, Lord, and he had them jackhammer blues.
   Jackhammer man from a jackhammer town.
   I can hammer on a hammer till the sun goes down.
   Lord, Lord, well, I got them jackhammer blues.

4. I hammered on the boulder, hammered on the butte;
   Columbia River on a five mile chute.
   Lord, Lord, and he had them jackhammer blues.
   Workin' on the Bonneville, hammered all night
   A tryin' to bring the people some electric light.
   Lord, Lord, well, I got them jackhammer blues.

5. I hammered on Bonneville, Coulee too.
   Always broke when my job was through.
   Lord, Lord, and he had them jackhammer blues.
   I hammered on the river from sun to sun,
   Fifteen million salmon run.
   Lord, Lord, well, I got them jackhammer blues.

6. I hammered in the rain, I hammered in the dust.
   I hammered in the best and I hammered in the worst.
   Lord, Lord, and he had them jackhammer blues.
   I got a jackhammer gal just as sweet as pie,
   And I'm a gonna hammer till the day I die.
   Lord, Lord, well, I got them jackhammer blues.

Jesus Christ

Words and Music by Woody Guthrie
Melody based on a traditional theme

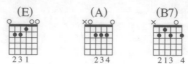

Capo II

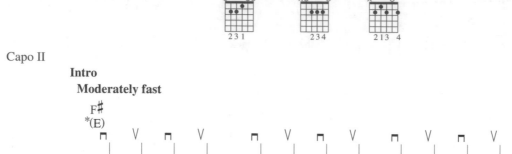

Intro
Moderately fast

1. Je - sus

* Symbols in parentheses represent chord names respective to capoed guitar.
Symbols above reflect actual sounding chords.

Verse

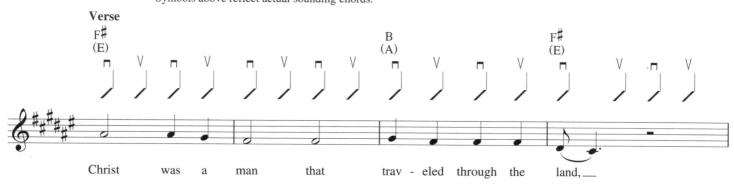

Christ was a man that trav - eled through the land, ___

hard - work - ing man and brave. ___ He

said to the rich, "Give your goods ___ to the poor," ___ so they

laid Je - sus Christ in His grave. ___

Chorus

Yes, Je - sus was a man, a

car - pen - ter by hand, His fol - low - ers true and

brave. One dir - ty cow - ard called

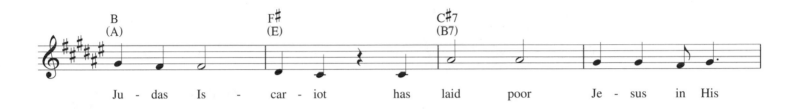

Ju - das Is - car - iot has laid poor Je - sus in His

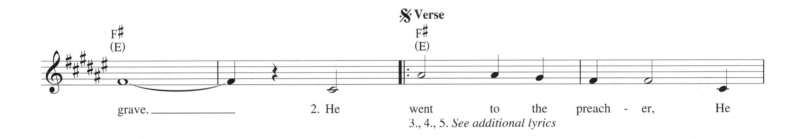

𝄋 Verse

grave. 2. He went to the preach - er, He

3., 4., 5. *See additional lyrics*

went to the sher - iff, told them all the

same. "Sell all of your jew - el - ry and

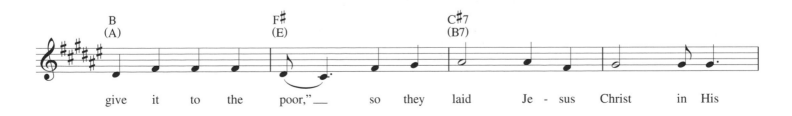

give it to the poor," so they laid Je - sus Christ in His

Additional Lyrics

3. When Jesus came to town, the working folks around
   Believed what He did say.
   The bankers and the preachers they nailed Him on a cross,
   And they laid Jesus Christ in His grave.

4. Well, the people held their breath when they heard about His death;
   Ev'rybody wondered why.
   It was the landlord and the soldiers that He hired
   That nailed Jesus Christ in the sky.

5. This song was made in New York City,
   Of a rich mans, and preachers, and slaves.
   If Jesus was to preach like He preached in Galilee,
   They would lay Jesus Christ in His grave.

Chorus Yes, Jesus was a man and a carpenter by hand,
   His followers true and brave.
   One dirty coward called Judas Iscariot
   Has layed poor Jesus in His grave.

Pastures of Plenty

Words and Music by Woody Guthrie

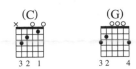

Capo II

Moderately **Verse**

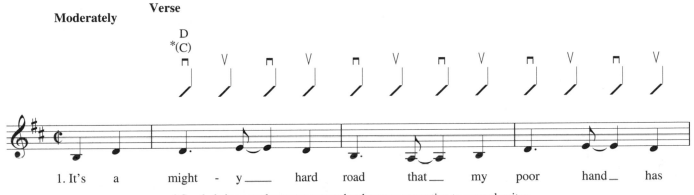

1. It's a might-y ___ hard road that ___ my poor hand ___ has

* Symbols in parentheses represent chord names respective to capoed guitar.
Symbols above reflect actual sounding chords.

hoed. My poor feet has

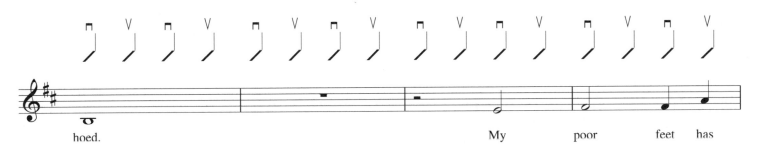

trav-eled a hot dust-y road. ___

___ Out of ___ your dust bowl ___ and

west-ward ___ we rolled, and your des-ert ___ was hot, and your

moun - tains___ was cold._____ 2. I

Verse
D
(C)

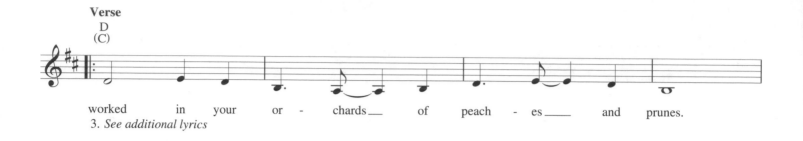

worked   in   your   or -   chards___   of   peach - es____   and   prunes.
3. *See additional lyrics*

Slept   on   the   ground___   in   the   light   of _____   your

moon._____   On   the   edge   of _____   your

cit - y   you've   seen   us _____   and   then,   we   come   with   the

1.

dust   and   we   go   with   the   wind._____

2.

3. Cal - i - wine._____   4. Green

30

Verse

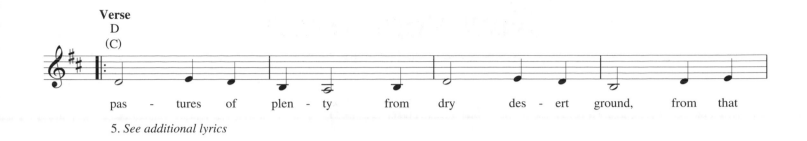

pas - tures of plen - ty from dry des - ert ground, from that

5. *See additional lyrics*

Grand Cou - lee Dam___ where the wat - er_____ runs down.

Ev' - ry state in_____ this un - ion us mi - grants___ have

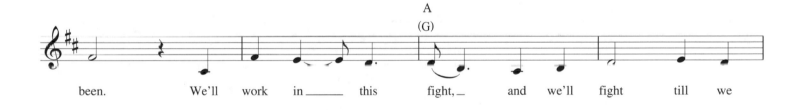

been. We'll work in_____ this fight,___ and we'll fight till we

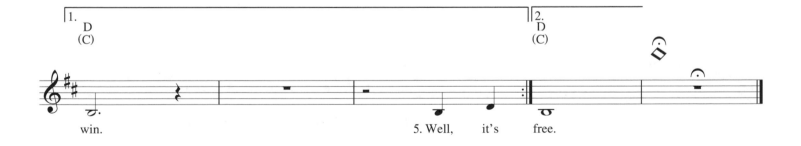

win.   5. Well, it's free.

Additional Lyrics

3. California and Arizona, I make all your crops.
   And it's north up to Oregon to gather your hops.
   Dig the beets from your ground, cut the grapes from your vine,
   To set on your table your light sparkling wine.

5. Well, it's always we ramble, that river and I.
   All along your green valley I'll work till I die.
   My land I'll defend with my life, if it be,
   'Cause my pastures of plenty must always be free.

New York Town

Words and Music by Woody Guthrie

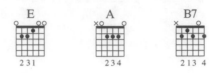

Intro
Moderately

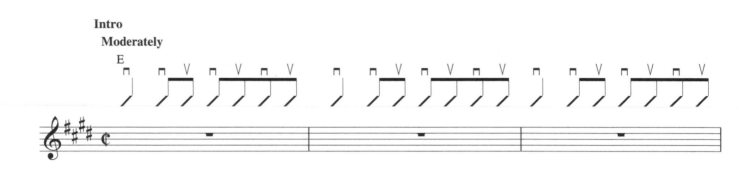

Verse

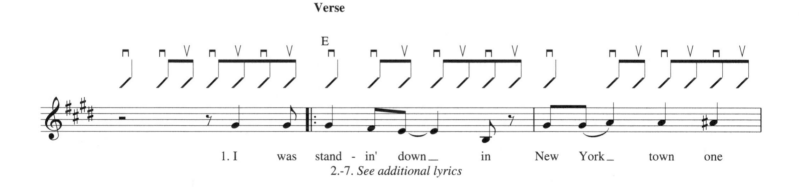

1. I was stand - in' down_ in New York_ town one
2.-7. See additional lyrics

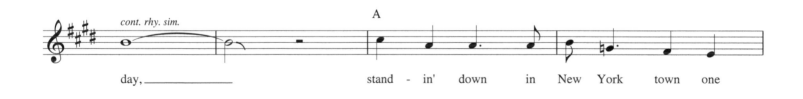

day, _____ stand - in' down in New York town one

day. I was stand - in' down_ in

New York town one day, sing - in' hey,

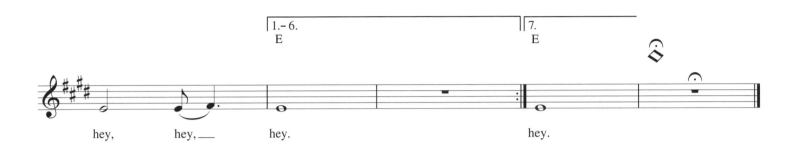

hey, hey,— hey. hey.

Additional Lyrics

2. I was broke, I didn't have a dime.
   I was broke, I didn't have a dime.
   Yes sir, I was broke, I didn't have a dime.
   Singin' hey, hey, hey, hey.

3. Ev'ry good man gets a little hard luck sometimes.
   Ev'ry good man gets a little hard luck sometimes.
   Ev'ry good man gets a little hard luck sometimes.
   Singin' hey, hey, hey, hey.

4. Down and out, he ain't got a dime.
   Down and out and a he ain't got a dime.
   Gets down and out and he ain't got a dime.
   Singin' hey, hey, hey, hey.

5. I'm a gonna ride that new mornin' railroad.
   I'm gonna ride that new mornin' train,
   Yes sir, I'm gonna ride that new mornin' train.
   Singin' hey, hey, hey, hey.

6. Hey, hey, hey, hey.
   Ho, ho, ho, ho, ho.
   Ho, ho, ho, ho, ho.
   Singin' hey, hey, hey, hey.

7. Never comin' back to this man's town again.
   Never comin' back to this man's town again.
   Never comin' back to this man's town again.
   Singin' hey, hey, hey, hey.

Ramblin' Round

Music based on "Goodnight, Irene" by Huddie Ledbetter and John Lomax
Words by Woody Guthrie

1. Ram - blin' a - round your cit - y, ____ ram - blin' a - round your

2.-6. *See additional lyrics*

* Symbols in parentheses represent chord names respective to capoed guitar.
Symbols above reflect actual sounding chords.

town. I nev - er see a friend I know ____ as

I go ram - blin' a - round, boys, ____ as I go ram - blin' a -

round.   2. My   round.

Additional Lyrics

2. My sweetheart and my parents
   I left in my old home town.
   I'm out to do the best I can
   As I go ramblin' around, boys,
   As I go ramblin' around.

3. The peach trees they are loaded,
   And the limbs are a bendin' down.
   I pick 'em all day for a dollar, boys,
   As I go ramblin' around,
   As I go ramblin' around.

4. Sometimes the fruit gets rotten,
   Falls down on the ground.
   There's a hungry mouth for ev'ry peach
   As I go ramblin' around, boys,
   As I go ramblin' around.

5. I wish that I could marry;
   I wished I could settle down.
   But I can't save a penny, boys,
   As I go ramblin' around,
   As I go ramblin' around.

6. My mother prayed that I would be
   A man of some renown.
   But I am just a refugee,
   As I go ramblin' around, boys,
   As I go ramblin' around.

Riding in My Car

Words and Music by Woody Guthrie

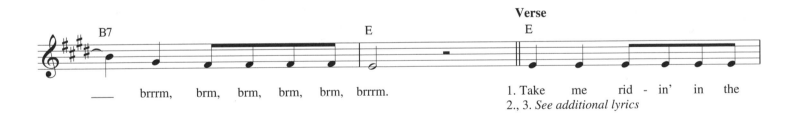

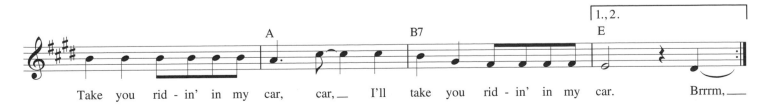

Additional Lyrics

2. Click clack, open up a door girls.
   Click clack, open up a door boys.
   Front door, back door, clickety clack;
   Take you ridin' in my car.

3. Climb, climb, rattle on a front seat;
   Spree I spraddle on the back seat.
   Turn my key, step on the starter.
   Take you ridin' in my car.

8. I'm gonna let you blow the horn.
   I'm gonna let you blow the horn.
   A-oorah, a-oorah, a-oorah.
   Well, I'll take you ridin' in my car.

Roll On, Columbia

Music based on "Goodnight, Irene" by Huddie Ledbetter and John Lomax
Words by Woody Guthrie

Capo II

Intro
Moderately

* Symbols in parentheses represent chord names respective to capoed guitar.
  Symbols above reflect actual sounding chords.

Verse

cont. rhy. sim.

1. Green Doug-las firs where the wa-ter cut through.
2. *See additional lyrics*
3. *Instrumental*

Down her wild mountains and canyons she flew.

Can-a-di-an Northwest to the ocean so blue, it's

To Coda

roll on, Columbia, roll on.

Chorus

Roll on, _____ Co - lum - bia, roll on. Roll

on, _____ Co - lum - bia, roll on. Your pow - er is

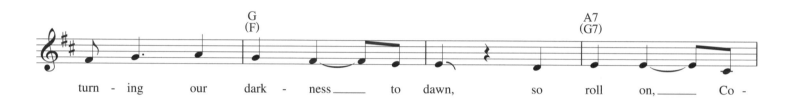

turn - ing our dark - ness _____ to dawn, so roll on, _____ Co -

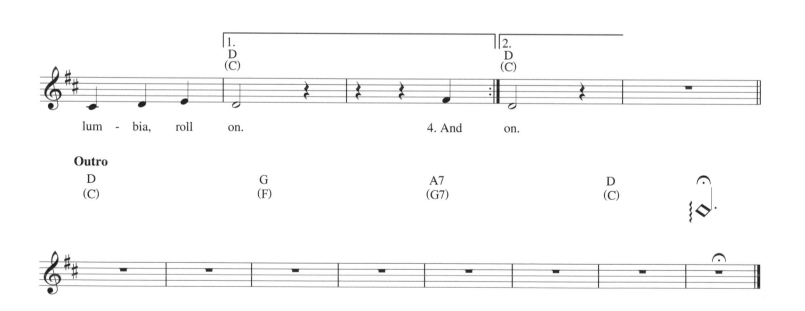

lum - bia, roll on. 4. And on.

Outro

Additional Lyrics

2. Tom Jefferson's vision would not let him rest;
   An empire he saw in the Pacific Northwest.
   Sent Lewis and Clark and they did the rest,
   So roll on, Columbia, roll on.

4. And up on the river is the Grand Coulee Dam,
   The mightiest thing ever built by man.
   To run the great factories and water the land,
   It's roll on, Columbia, roll on.

Vigilante Man

Words and Music by Woody Guthrie

Capo II

Intro
Moderately

* Symbols in parentheses represent chord names respective to capoed guitar.
  Symbols above reflect actual sounding chords.

Verse

1. Have you seen_____ that vig - i - lan - te man?

Have you seen that vig - i - lan - te _____ man?

Have you seen that vig - i - lan - te man?_

I've___ been a hear - in' his name all o - ver the land.

Verse

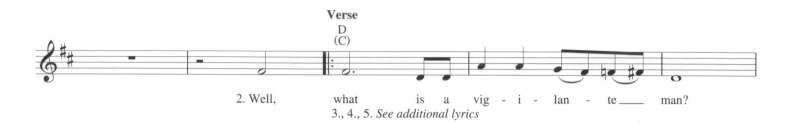

2. Well, what is a vig - i - lan - te___ man?
3., 4., 5. *See additional lyrics*

Tell me what is a vig - i - lan - te___ man?

Has he got a gun and a club in his hand? Is

|1., 2., 3.|

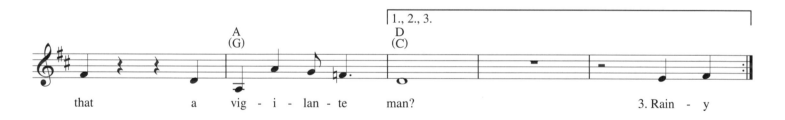

that a vig - i - lan - te man? 3. Rain - y

|4.| **Harmonica Solo**

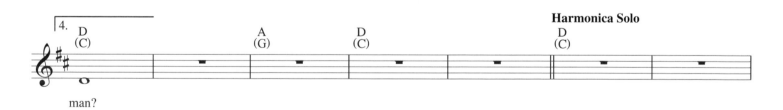

man?

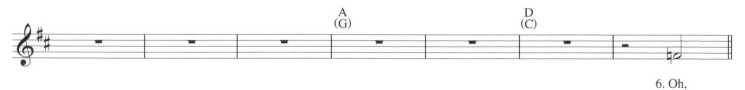

6. Oh,

Verse

why does a vig - i - lan - te man,

7. See additional lyrics

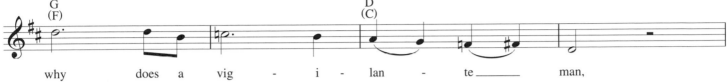

why does a vig - i - lan - te _____ man,

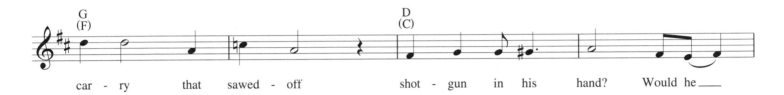

car - ry that sawed - off shot - gun in his hand? Would he ____

shoot his broth - er and sis - /ter down?_ 7. I _____

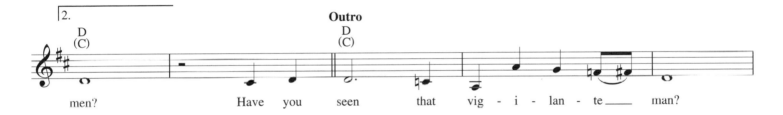

Outro

men? Have you seen that vig - i - lan - te _____ man?

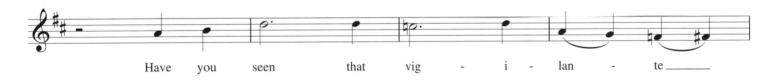

Have you seen that vig - i - lan - te _____

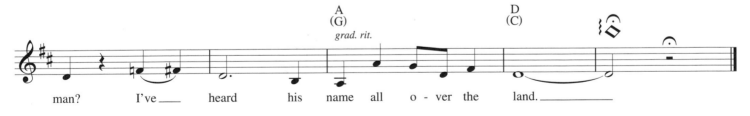

grad. rit.

man? I've ____ heard his name all o - ver the land. _____

Additional Lyrics

3. Rainy night down in the engine house;
   Sleepin' just as still as a mouse.
   Man come along and he chased us out in the rain.
   Was that a vigilante man?

4. Stormy days we'd pass the time away,
   Sleepin' in some good warm place.
   Man come along and we give him a little race.
   Was that a vigilante man?

5. Preacher Casey was just a workin' man,
   And he said, unite all you workin' men.
   Killed him in the river, some strange man.
   Was that a vigilante man?

7. I rambled around from town to town.
   I rambled around from town to town.
   And they herded us around like a wild herd of cattle.
   Was that the vigilante men?

So Long It's Been Good to Know Yuh
(Dusty Old Dust)

Words and Music by Woody Guthrie

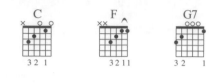

Intro
Moderately

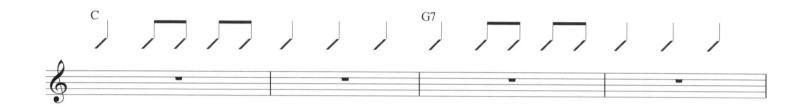

1. I've

Verse

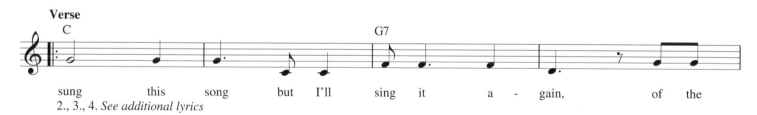

sung   this   song   but   I'll   sing   it   a - gain,   of the
2., 3., 4. See additional lyrics

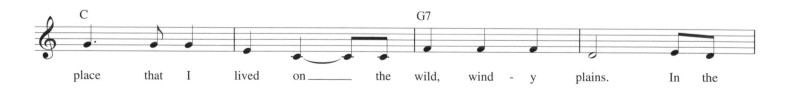

place   that   I   lived   on _____ the   wild,   wind - y   plains.   In the

month   called   A - pril,   coun - ty   called _____ Gray,   and

here's   what   all   of   the   peo - ple   there   say:

Chorus

So   long,   it's   been   good   to   know   ya.

So   long,   it's   been   good   to   know   ya.

So   long,   it's   been   good   to   know   ya.   This

dust - y   old   dust   is   a   get - tin'   my   home,   and   I've

1., 2., 3.

got   to   be   drift - in'   a - long.   2. A

4.

Verse

long.   5. Now,   the   tel - e - phone   rang   and   it

jumped   off   the   wall.   That   was   the   preach - er   a

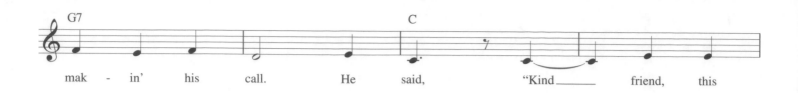

mak - in' his call. He said, "Kind ____ friend, this

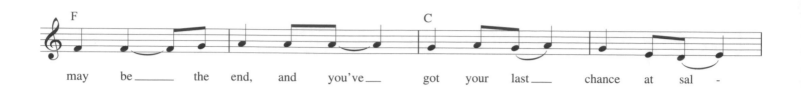

may be ____ the end, and you've ____ got your last ____ chance at sal -

va - tion of ____ sin." 6. The

Verse

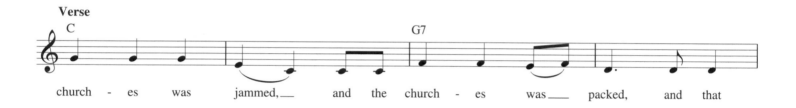

church - es was jammed, ____ and the church - es was ____ packed, and that

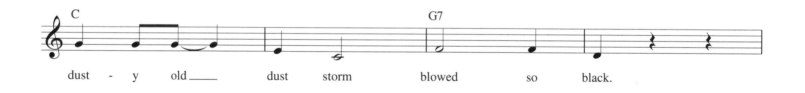

dust - y old ____ dust storm blowed so black.

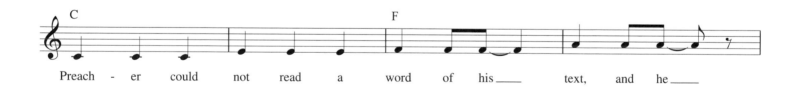

Preach - er could not read a word of his ____ text, and he ____

fold - ed his ____ specs, and he ____ took up ____ col - lec - tion. Said,

Outro-Chorus

so long, been good to know ____ ya.

46

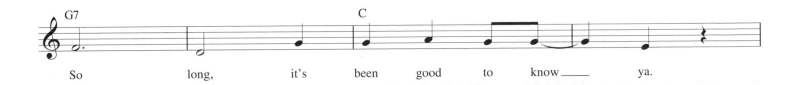

So long, it's been good to know ___ ya.

So long, it's been good to know ___ ya. This ___

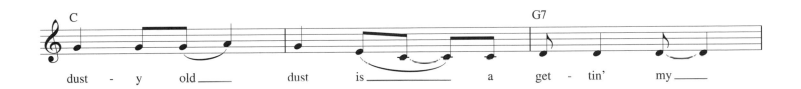

dust - y old ___ dust is ___ a get - tin' my ___

home, ___

and I've ___

grad. rit.

got to be drift - in' a - long.

Additional Lyrics

2. A dust storm hit, and it hit like thunder.
   It dusted us over, and it covered us under.
   Blocked out the traffic and blocked out the sun.
   Straight for home all the people did run.
   Singin'...

3. We talked of the end of the world, and then
   We'd sing a song and then sing it again.
   We'd sit for an hour and not say a word,
   And then these words would be heard:

4. Sweethearts sat in the dark and sparked.
   They hugged and kissed in that dusty old dark.
   They sighed and cried, hugged and kissed.
   Instead of marriage they talked like this:
   Honey,...

Talking Dust Bowl

Words and Music by Woody Guthrie

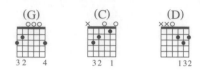

Capo II

Verse

Moderately

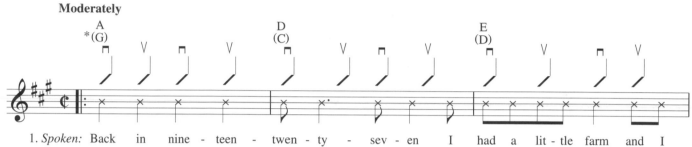

1. *Spoken:* Back in nine - teen - twen - ty - sev - en I had a lit - tle farm and I
2.-6. *See additional lyrics*

* Symbols in parentheses represent chord names respective to capoed guitar.
  Symbols above reflect actual sounding chords.

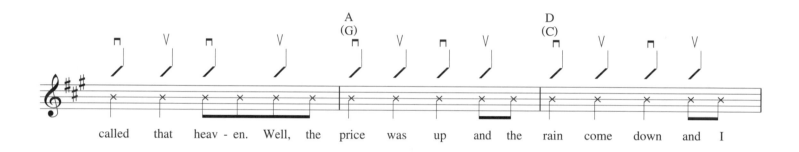

called that heav - en. Well, the price was up and the rain come down and I

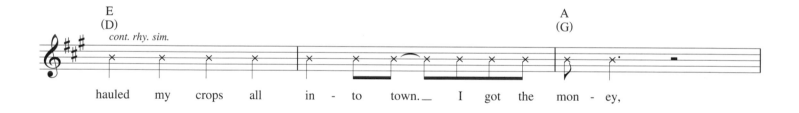

hauled my crops all in - to town.— I got the mon - ey,

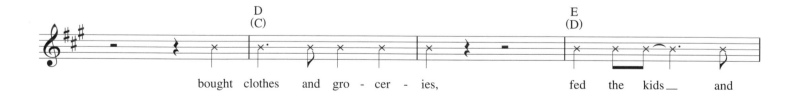

bought clothes and gro - cer - ies, fed the kids — and

raised _____ a fam - i - ly.

Outro-Verse

Spoken: Al - ways have fig - ured that if it had been just a lit - tle bit___

___ thin - ner, some of these here pol - i -

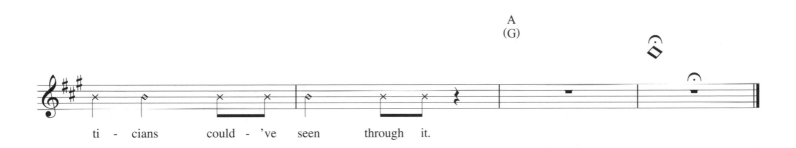

ti - cians could - 've seen through it.

Additional Lyrics

2. Rain quit and the wind got high,
   And a black old dust storm filled the sky.
   And I swapped my farm for a Ford machine,
   And I poured it full of this gasoline.
   And I started. Rocking and a rolling.
   Over the mountains out towards the old peach bowl.

3. Way up yonder on a mountain road,
   I had a hot motor and a heavy loud.
   I was going pretty fast, I wasn't even stoppin',
   A bouncin' up and down like popcorn poppin'.
   Had a breakdown, and sort of a nervous bust-down of some kind.
   There was a feller there, a mechanic feller, said it was engine trouble.

4. Way up yonder on a mountain curve,
   It's a way up yonder in the piney wood,
   And I give that rollin' Ford a shove,
   And I was gonna coast as far as I could.
   Commenced coastin'; pickin' up speed.
   There was a hairpin turn... I didn't make it.

5. Man alive, I'm a tellin' you,
   The fiddles and the guitars really flew.
   That Ford took off like a flyin' squirrel,
   And it flew halfway around the world.
   Scattered wives and childrens
   All over the side of that mountain.

6. We got out to the West Coast broke,
   So dad gum hungry I thought I'd croak.
   And I bummed up a spud or two,
   And my wife fixed up a tater stew.
   We poured the kids full of it. Mighty thin stew though.
   You could read the magazine right through it.

This Land Is Your Land

Words and Music by Woody Guthrie

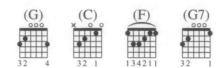

Capo III

Intro
Moderately

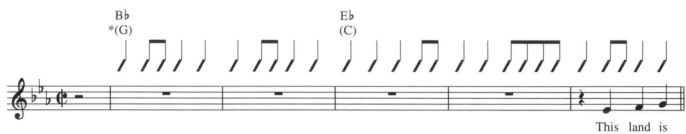

*Symbols in parentheses represent chord names respective to capoed guitar.
Symbols above reflect actual sounding chords.

Chorus

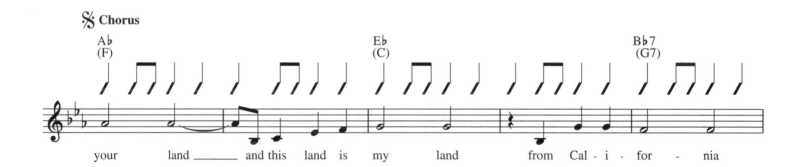

your land _____ and this land is my land from Cal - i - for - nia

to the New York is - land. From the red-wood for - est to the Gulf Stream wat - ers, ____

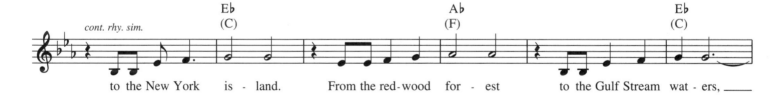

3rd time, To Coda ⊕

____ this land was made _ for you and me. 1. As I ___ was

Verse

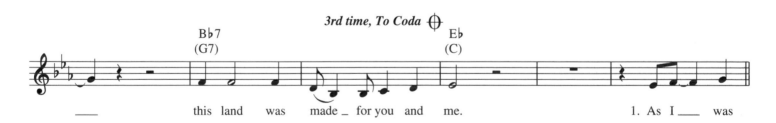

walk - ing _____ that rib - bon of high - way, I saw a - bove me
ram - bled _____ and I fol-lowed my foot - steps to the spar - kling sands of

3. - 6. *See additional lyrics*

Additional Lyrics

3. When the sun came shining, and I was strolling,
   And the wheat fields waving and the dust clouds rolling,
   As the fog was lifting a voice was chanting:
   "This land was made for you and me."

4. As I went walking, I saw a sign there,
   And on the sign it said "No Trespassing."
   But on the other side it didn't say nothing.
   That side was made for you and me.

5. In the shadow of the steeple I saw my people,
   By the relief office I seen my people;
   As they stood there hungry, I stood there asking:
   Is this land made for you and me?

6. Nobody living can ever stop me,
   As I go walking that freedom highway;
   Nobody living can ever make me turn back.
   This land was made for you and me.

Tom Joad

Words and Music by Woody Guthrie
Melody based on a traditional theme

* Symbols in parentheses represent chord names respective to capoed guitar.
Symbols above reflect actual sounding chords.

1. Tom Joad got out of the old __ Mc-Al-es-ter
2.-17. *See additional lyrics*

pen, there he got his __ pa-role.

Af-ter four long years on a man kill-in' charge, __

__ Tom Joad come a walk-in' down the road, poor __

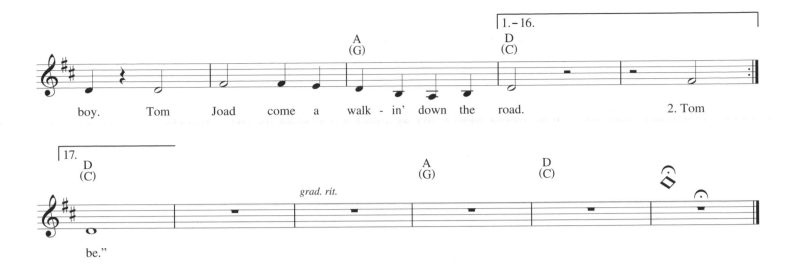

boy.   Tom   Joad   come   a   walk - in'   down   the   road.   2. Tom

be."

Additional Lyrics

2. Tom Joad he met a truck drivin' man,
   There he caught him a ride.
   He said, "I just got loose from McAlester pen
   On a charge called homicide,
   A charge called homicide."

3. That truck rolled away in a cloud of dust,
   Tommy turned his face toward home.
   He met Preacher Casey and they had a little drink,
   But they found that his family they was gone.
   He found that his family they was gone.

4. He found his mother's old-fashioned shoe,
   Found his daddy's hat.
   And he found little Muley and Muley said,
   "They've been tractored out by the cats.
   They've been tractored out by the cats."

5. Tom Joad walked down to the neighbor's farm,
   Found his family.
   They took Preacher Casey and loaded in a car.
   And his mother said, "We've got to get away."
   His mother said, "We've got to get away."

6. Now the twelve of the Joads made a mighty heavy load,
   But Grandpa Joad did cry.
   He picked up a handful of land in his hand,
   Said, "I'm stayin' with the farm till I die.
   Yes, I'm stayin' with the farm till I die."

7. They fed him short ribs and coffee and soothing syrup.
   And Grandpa Joad did die.
   They buried Grandpa Joad by the side of the road,
   Grandma on the California side.
   They buried Grandma on the California side.

8. They stood on a mountain and they looked to the west,
   And it looked like the promised land.
   That bright green valley with a river running through.
   There was work for ev'ry single hand, they thought.
   There was work for ev'ry single hand.

9. The Joads rode away to the jungle camp;
   There they cooked a stew.
   And the hungry little kids of the jungle camp
   Said, "We'd like to have some too."
   Said, "We'd like to have some too."

10. Now a deputy sheriff fired loose at a man,
    Shot a woman in the back.
    Before he could take his aim again,
    Preacher Casey dropped him in his track, poor boy.
    Preacher Casey dropped him in his track.

11. They handcuffed to Casey and they took him to jail,
    And then he got away.
    And he met Tom Joad on the old river bridge,
    And these few words he did say, poor boy,
    These few words he did say:

12. "I preached for the Lord a mighty long time;
    Preached about the rich and the poor.
    Us workin' folks is all get together
    'Cause we ain't got a chance anymore.
    We ain't got a chance anymore."

13. Now the deputies come and Tom and Casey run
    To the bridge where the water run down.
    But the vigilante thugs hit Casey with a club,
    They laid Preacher Casey on the ground, poor Casey.
    They laid Preacher Casey on the ground.

14. Tom Joad he grabbed that deputy's club,
    Hit him over the head.
    Tom Joad took flight in the dark, rainy night,
    And a deputy and a preacher lyin' dead, two men.
    A deputy and a preacher lyin' dead.

15. Tom run back where his mother was asleep,
    He woke her up out of bed.
    Then he kissed goodbye to the mother that he loved.
    Said what Preacher Casey said, Tom Joad,
    He said what Preacher Casey said...

16. "Ev'rybody might be just one big soul.
    Well, it looks that a way to me.
    Ev'rywhere that you look in the day or night,
    That's where I'm a gonna be, Ma.
    That's where I'm a gonna be."

17. "Wherever little children are hungry and cry,
    Wherever people ain't free,
    Wherever men are fightin' for their rights,
    That's where I'm a gonna be, Ma.
    That's where I'm a gonna be."

Woody Guthrie DVDs, Videos and Books

DVD/VHS

Bound for Glory, 1976 Hal Ashby, director. United Artists film-MGM video & DVD

Folkways: A Vision Shared/Tribute to Woody Guthrie and Leadbelly, 1988 Robbie Robertson, narrator.
  Ginger Group Productions. Sony DVD

Man in the Sand (The Making of "Mermaid Avenue"), 2001Billy Bragg & Wilco.
  A Union Production film for BBC and NVC Arts. Rykovision DVD

Roll On Columbia/Woody Guthrie & the Bonneville Power Administration, 2000 University of Oregon Knight Library
  Media Services VHS

This Land Is Your Land: The Animated Kids' Songs of Woody Guthrie, 1997 Guthrie/Calico Productions.
  Family Home Entertainment DVD

Woody Guthrie: This Machine Kills Fascists, 2005 Documentary. Snapper UK DVD

BOOKS

Bray, Thelma — 2001 *Reflections: The Life and Times of Woody Guthrie.* Thelma Bray (Pampa, TX).

Brower, Steven and Guthrie, Nora — 2005 *Woody Guthrie; Artworks.* Rizzoli.

Christensen, Bonnie — 2001 *Woody Guthrie; Poet of the People.* Alfred A. Knopf.

Coombs, Karen Mueller — 2002 *Woody Guthrie: America's Folksinger.* Carolrhoda Books, Inc. (Lerner Publishing Group).

Cray, Ed — 2005 *Ramblin' Man: The Life and Times of Woody Guthrie.* W. W. Norton & Co.

Guthrie, Woody — 1943 *Bound for Glory.* E. P. Dutton & Co., Inc.

1976 *Seeds of Man: An Experience Lived and Dreamed.* University of Nebraska Press.

1990 *Pastures of Plenty: A Self-Portrait.* Edited by Dave Marsh and Harold Leventhal. Harper Collins.

Guthrie, Woody and Frazee, Maria — 2004 *New Baby Train.* Little, Brown and Company.

Guthrie, Woody and Jakobsen, Kathy — 1998 *This Land Is Your Land.* Little, Brown and Company.

Guthrie, Woody and Radunsky, Vladimir — 2000 *Bling Blang.* Candlewick Press.

2000 *Howdi Do.* Candlewick Press.

2001 *My Dolly.* Candlewick Press.

Klein, Joe — 1980 *Woody Guthrie: A Life.* Delta/Dell Publishing, Random House, Inc.

Longhi, Jim — 1997 *Woody, Cisco & Me: Seamen Three in the Merchant Marine.* University of Illinois Press.

Neimark, Anne E. — 2002 *There Ain't Nobody That Can Sing Like Me: The Life of Woody Guthrie.* Atheneum.

Partridge, Elizabeth — 2002 *This Land Was Made For You And Me: The Life and Songs of Woody Guthrie.* Viking Juvenile.

Santelli, Robert and Davidson, Emily — 1999 *Hard Travelin': The Life and Legacy of Woody Guthrie.* Wesleyan University Press.

Yates, Janelle — 1995 *Woody Guthrie: American Balladeer.* Ward Hill Press.

SONGBOOKS

Guthrie, Woody — 1991 *Roll On Columbia: The Columbia River Collection.* Bill Murlin, editor. Sing Out Publications

1994 *Woody Guthrie Songbook.* Judy Bell and Nora Guthrie, editors. TRO-Ludlow Music, Inc.

2002 *Best of Woody Guthrie: Strum It Guitar.* Mick O'Brien, arranger. TRO-Ludlow Music, Inc.

Recordings by Woody Guthrie

Asch Recordings Box Set, Vol. 1-4 (Smithsonian Folkways)
 This Land Is Your Land, Vol. 1
 Muleskinner Blues, Vol. 2
 Hard Travelin', Vol. 3
 Buffalo Skinners, Vol. 4
Ballads of Sacco and Vanzetti (Rounder)
Columbia River Collection (Rounder)
Dust Bowl Ballads (Buddha)
Folkways: The Original Vision (Smithsonian Folkways)
Library of Congress Recordings (Rounder)
Long Ways To Travel (Smithsonian Folkways)
Nursery Days (Smithsonian Folkways)
Songs To Grow On For Mother And Child (Smithsonian Folkways)
Struggle (Smithsonian Folkways)
Woody Guthrie Sings Folk Songs (Smithsonian Folkways)

Woody Guthrie Recordings by Other Artists

Billy Bragg & Wilco: Mermaid Avenue (Elektra)
Billy Bragg & Wilco: Mermaid Avenue, Vol. 2 (Elektra)
Ramblin' Jack Elliott: Hard Travelin' (Fantasy)
Cisco Houston: Best of the Vanguard Years (Vanguard)
Cisco Houston: The Folkways Years (Smithsonian Folkways)
Klezmatics: Happy Joyous Hanukkah (Jewish Music Group)
Klezmatics: Wonder Wheel (Jewish Music Group)
Country Joe McDonald: Thinking of Woody Guthrie (Vanguard)
Joel Rafael: Woodeye (Inside Recordings)
Joel Rafael: Woodyboye (Appleseed)
James Talley: Woody Guthrie and Songs of My Oklahoma Home (Cimarron)
Vanaver Caravan: Pastures of Plenty (Vanaver Caravan)
Various Artists: Daddy-O-Daddy/Rare Family Songs of Woody Guthrie (Rounder)
Various Artists: Hard Travelin' film soundtrack (Rising Son)
Various Artists: 'Til We Outnumber 'Em 1996 Rock & Roll Hall of Fame and Museum tribute to Woody Guthrie
 (Righteous Babe)
Various Artists: A Tribute to Woody Guthrie/Carnegie Hall 1968. Hollywood Bowl 1970 (Warner)
Various Artists: Woody Guthrie's American Song Cast Album (www.woodyguthrie.org)
Wenzel: Ticky Tock/Wenzel Sings Woody Guthrie (Contrar)
Z-Joe & the Dustbowlers: A Woody Zombie Hootenanny (Safety Records)

STRUM IT GUITAR

· AUTHENTIC CHORDS · ORIGINAL KEYS · COMPLETE SONGS ·

The *Strum It* series lets players strum the chords and sing along with their favorite hits. Each song has been selected because it can be played with regular open chords, barre chords, or other moveable chord types. Guitarists can simply play the rhythm, or play and sing along through the entire song. All songs are shown in their original keys complete with chords, strum patterns, melody and lyrics. Wherever possible, the chord voicings from the recorded versions are notated.

Acoustic Classics 00699238 / $10.95
21 classics: And I Love Her • Barely Breathing • Free Fallin' • Maggie May • Mr. Jones • Only Wanna Be with You • Patience • Wonderful Tonight • Yesterday • more.

The Beach Boys' Greatest Hits 00699357 / $12.95
19 tunes: Barbara Ann • California Girls • Fun, Fun, Fun • Good Vibrations • Help Me Rhonda • I Get Around • Surfer Girl • Surfin' U.S.A. • Wouldn't It Be Nice • more.

The Beatles Favorites 00699249 / $14.95
23 Beatles hits: Can't Buy Me Love • Eight Days a Week • Hey Jude • Let It Be • She Loves You • Yesterday • You've Got to Hide Your Love Away • and more.

Best of Contemporary Christian 00699531 / $12.95
20 CCM favorites: Awesome God • Butterfly Kisses • El Shaddai • Father's Eyes • I Could Sing of Your Love Forever • Jesus Freak • The Potter's Hand • and more.

Best of Steven Curtis Chapman 00699530 / $12.95
16 top hits: For the Sake of the Call • Heaven in the Real World • His Strength Is Perfect • I Will Be Here • More to This Life • Signs of Life • What Kind of Joy • more.

Very Best of Johnny Cash 00699514 / $9.95
17 songs: A Boy Named Sue • Daddy Sang Bass • Folsom Prison Blues • I Walk the Line • The Man in Black • Orange Blossom Special • Ring of Fire • and more.

Celtic Guitar Songbook 00699265 / $9.95
35 songs: Cockles and Mussels • Danny Boy • The Irish Washerwoman • Kerry Dance • Killarney • My Wild Irish Rose • Sailor's Hornpipe • and more.

Christmas Songs for Guitar 00699247 / $9.95
40 favorites: Frosty the Snow Man • Grandma Got Run Over by a Reindeer • I'll Be Home for Christmas • Rockin' Around the Christmas Tree • Silver Bells • more.

Christmas Songs with 3 Chords 00699487 / $8.95
30 all-time favorites: Angels We Have Heard on High • Away in a Manger • Here We Come A-Wassailing • Jolly Old St. Nicholas • Silent Night • Up on the Housetop • more.

Very Best of Eric Clapton 00699560 / $12.95
20 songs: Change the World • For Your Love • I Shot the Sheriff • Layla • My Father's Eyes • Tears in Heaven • White Room • Wonderful Tonight • and more.

Country Strummin' 00699119 / $8.95
Features 24 songs: Achy Breaky Heart • Blue • A Broken Wing • Gone Country • I Fall to Pieces • She and I • Unchained Melody • What a Crying Shame • and more.

Jim Croce – Classic Hits 00699269 / $10.95
22 great songs: Bad, Bad Leroy Brown • I'll Have to Say I Love You in a Song • Operator (That's Not the Way It Feels) • Time in a Bottle • and more.

Very Best of John Denver 00699488 / $12.95
20 top hits: Leaving on a Jet Plane • Rocky Mountain High • Sunshine on My Shoulders • Take Me Home, Country Roads • Thank God I'm a Country Boy • more.

Neil Diamond 00699593 / $12.95
28 classics: America • Cracklin' Rosie • Forever in Blue Jeans • Hello Again • I'm a Believer • Love on the Rocks • Song Sung Blue • Sweet Caroline • and more.

Disney Favorites 00699171 / $10.95
34 Disney favorites: Can You Feel the Love Tonight • Cruella De Vil • Friend Like Me • It's a Small World • Under the Sea • Whistle While You Work • and more.

Disney Greats 00699172 / $10.95
39 classics: Beauty and the Beast • Colors of the Wind • Go the Distance • Heigh-Ho • Kiss the Girl • When You Wish Upon a Star • Zip-A-Dee-Doo-Dah • and more.

Best of The Doors 00699177 / $10.95
25 Doors favorites: Been Down So Long • Hello I Love You Won't You Tell Me Your Name? • Light My Fire • Riders on the Storm • Touch Me • and more.

Favorite Songs with 3 Chords 00699112 / $8.95
27 popular songs: All Shook Up • Boot Scootin' Boogie • Great Balls of Fire • Lay Down Sally • Semi-Charmed Life • Twist and Shout • Wooly Bully • and more.

Favorite Songs with 4 Chords 00699270 / $8.95
22 tunes: Beast of Burden • Don't Be Cruel • Gloria • I Fought the Law • La Bamba • Last Kiss • Let Her Cry • Love Stinks • Peggy Sue • 3 AM • Wild Thing • and more.

Fireside Sing-Along 00699273 / $8.95
25 songs: Edelweiss • Leaving on a Jet Plane • Take Me Home, Country Roads • Teach Your Children • This Land Is Your Land • You've Got a Friend • and more.

Folk Favorites 00699517 / $8.95
42 traditional favorites: Camptown Races • Clementine • Danny Boy • My Old Kentucky Home • Rock-A-My Soul • Scarborough Fair • and more.

Irving Berlin's God Bless America® 00699508 / $9.95
25 patriotic anthems: America, the Beautiful • Battle Hymn of the Republic • God Bless America • The Star Spangled Banner • This Land Is Your Land • and more.

Great '50s Rock 00699187 / $9.95
28 hits: At the Hop • Blueberry Hill • Bye Bye Love • Hound Dog • Rock Around the Clock • That'll Be the Day • and more.

Great '60s Rock 00699188 / $9.95
27 classic rock songs: And I Love Her • Gloria • Mellow Yellow • Return to Sender • Runaway • Surfin' U.S.A. • The Twist • Under the Boardwalk • Wild Thing • more.

Great '70s Rock 00699262 / $9.95
21 classic hits: Band on the Run • Lay Down Sally • Let It Be • Love Hurts • Ramblin' Man • Time for Me to Fly • Two Out of Three Ain't Bad • Wild World • and more.

Great '80s Rock 00699263 / $9.95
23 favorites: Centerfold • Free Fallin' • Got My Mind Set on You • Kokomo • Should I Stay or Should I Go • Uptown Girl • What I Like About You • and more.

Great '90s Rock 00699268 / $9.95
17 contemporary hits: If You Could Only See • Iris • Mr. Jones • Only Wanna Be with You • Tears in Heaven • Torn • The Way • You Were Meant for Me • and more.

Best of Woody Guthrie 00699496 / $12.95
20 songs: Do Re Mi • The Grand Coulee Dam • Roll On, Columbia • So Long It's Been Good to Know Yuh • This Land Is Your Land • Tom Joad • and more.

John Hiatt Collection 00699398 / $12.95
17 classics: Angel Eyes • Feels Like Rain • Have a Little Faith in Me • Riding with the King • Thing Called Love (Are You Ready for This Thing Called Love) • and more.

Hymn Favorites 00699271 / $9.95
Includes: Amazing Grace • Down by the Riverside • Holy, Holy, Holy • Just as I Am • Rock of Ages • What a Friend We Have in Jesus • and more.

Carole King Collection 00699234 / $12.95
20 songs: I Feel the Earth Move • It's Too Late • A Natural Woman • So Far Away • Tapestry • Will You Love Me Tomorrow • You've Got a Friend • and more.

Very Best of Dave Matthews Band 00699520 / $12.95
12 favorites: Ants Marching • Crash into Me • Crush • Don't Drink the Water • Everyday • The Space Between • Stay (Wasting Time) • What Would You Say • and more.

Sarah McLachlan 00699231 / $10.95
20 of Sarah's hits: Angel • Building a Mystery • I Will Remember You • Ice Cream • Sweet Surrender • more.

A Merry Christmas Songbook 00699211 / $8.95
51 holiday hits: Away in a Manger • Deck the Hall • Fum, Fum, Fum • The Holly and the Ivy • Jolly Old St. Nicholas • O Christmas Tree • and more!

More Favorite Songs with 3 Chords 00699532 / $8.95
27 great hits: Barbara Ann • Gloria • Hang on Sloopy • Hound Dog • La Bamba • Mony, Mony • Rock Around the Clock • Rock This Town • Rockin' Robin • and more.

Pop-Rock Guitar Favorites 00699088 / $8.95
31 songs: Angie • Brown Eyed Girl • Eight Days a Week • Free Bird • Gloria • Hey Jude • Let It Be • Maggie May • Wild Thing • Wonderful Tonight • and more.

Elvis! Greatest Hits 00699276 / $10.95
24 Elvis classics: All Shook Up • Always on My Mind • Can't Help Falling in Love • Hound Dog • It's Now or Never • Jailhouse Rock • Love Me Tender • and more.

Songs for Kids 00699616 / $9.95
28 fun favorites: Alphabet Song • Bingo • Frere Jacques • Kum Ba Yah • London Bridge • Old MacDonald • Pop Goes the Weasel • Yankee Doodle • more.

Best of George Strait 00699235 / $10.95
20 Strait hits: Adalida • All My Ex's Live in Texas • Carried Away • Does Fort Worth Ever Cross Your Mind • Right or Wrong • Write This Down • and more.

25 Country Standards 00699523 / $12.95
Includes: Always on My Mind • Amazed • Elvira • Friends in Low Places • Hey, Good Lookin' • Sixteen Tons • You Are My Sunshine • Your Cheatin' Heart • and more.

Best of Hank Williams Jr. 00699224 / $10.95
24 signature standards: All My Rowdy Friends Are Coming Over Tonight • Honky Tonkin' • There's a Tear in My Beer • Whiskey Bent and Hell Bound • and more.

Women of Rock 00699183 / $9.95
22 hits: Don't Speak • Give Me One Reason • I Don't Want to Wait • Insensitive • Lovefool • Stay • Torn • You Oughta Know • You Were Meant for Me • and more.

FOR MORE INFORMATION, SEE YOUR LOCAL MUSIC DEALER, OR WRITE TO:

HAL•LEONARD® CORPORATION
7777 W. BLUEMOUND RD. P.O. BOX 13819 MILWAUKEE, WI 53213

Visit Hal Leonard online at www.halleonard.com

Prices, contents & availability subject to change without notice.